D0343506

THE LITTLE BOOK OF MOMFULNESS

A NONEXPERT GUIDE TO IMPERFECT MOMHOOD

Sarah Ford

spruce

CONTENTS

Introduction

MOMFULNESS / *mom-full-ness* / **(noun):** derivation
of term *mindfulness*, brought into colloquial use during
the brief interest in mindfulness in the early 21st century.
  1 A state in which an individual mother attempts
to maintain her mindful attitude toward life while
dealing with the stresses and strains of motherhood
(see *mom* and *vain hope*); **2** A mental state achieved by
the acknowledgment and calm acceptance that perfect
motherhood is wholly unattainable (see *self-doubt*
and *stress*); **3** The quality or state of ordered disorder
that exists within the mind of every mother (see
chaos); **4** The practice of maintaining a nonjudgmental
view of those around one, and offering kindness and
compassion to all (see *self-deception*); **5** An attempt
to be not overly reactive or overwhelmed by the
sheer quantity of tasks a mother performs every
day (see *meltdown*).

The CoMOMndments

The darkest hour is just before bedtime

If cake be the food of sanity, eat on

When life gives you laundry, make Dad do it

She who naps last, naps longest

Behind every great mom there's a bar of chocolate

Beauty is in the eye of the crayon holder

Hell hath no fury like a woman cleaning

Take care of the odd socks, and the laundry will take care of itself

There's no
point crying
over spilt pee

All things
come to he
who gives
Mom a
nice gift

Wash up in
haste, bathe
at leisure

A bottle a
day keeps the
breakdown
away

A little
internet
shopping is
a dangerous
thing

Mighty
meals from
little carts
groweth

A mug in the
hand is worth
30 in the
dishwasher

A watched
microwave
never pings

Homework
is 1 percent
inspiration,
99 percent
mom

BE IN THE MOMENT

*really focus on those chores
to enjoy them to the full*

Mindful mom

Mindfulness (noun): a mental state achieved by focussing on the here and now; not letting the mind wander to the past or the future. To clear one's mind of the To-Do List, the weekly schedule, birthday calendar, playdates, weekly grocery shopping, baby clinic appointments, dropping the kids off at school, bag lunches, laundry basket... a state of mind rarely achieved by any human mother on Earth. But it's good to have a goal, right?

Be always in the moment...
Mom was always mindful when caring for her children, except for the time when she lost the little one in Ikea on Black Friday. She had only taken her eye off of him for a split second to examine the ingredients list on a package of meatballs.

Meditation before mediation

Let's meditate (no excuses now)

We all think we are too busy to do it, but a little meditation each day might just make us feel happier and increase our productivity. Meditation isn't just for celebrities, the rich, yogis, yoga mommies, and Buddhists. Anyone can do it, and you can even do it at home using household equipment.

So no need to worry about the humiliation of falling asleep in public. Just throw down a soft mat on a patch of sunlit floor while the baby is napping. Or failing that, lock yourself in the bathroom for ten minutes with your earplugs in and pray no one needs to go.

Meditation checklist

• Choose a good time (very funny).

• Put on your comfortable underpants.

• Sit up straight. No slouching.

• Breathe naturally and observe each breath as it comes in and goes out. Keep calm and try not to think about anything that will get your heart racing (like Ryan Gosling).

• Close your eyes to avoid distraction; no peeping or it won't work (so *that's* where Barbie's boyfriend Ken left his figure-hugging tank top).

• Focus your mind on your whole body and be aware of every part of you (don't obsess too much about your the parts that wobble).

• Smile and feel the calm washing over you like gentle waves on a sandy beach…("Wake up Mommy! You're snoring. I can't hear the TV!")

Mindful eating
Not to be confused with Mom's Always Eating

Momful eating (noun): To think about what you are eating, why you are eating it, where it came from, and experience the enjoyment of every mouthful. To provide one's family with a carefully thought-out, balanced meal (like serving a few frozen peas with the fried chicken nuggets), being grateful for what is put on the table (thank you, Colonel Saunders), and eating slowly to appreciate each mouthful. Mom usually wolfs it down while it's hot, before she is called away to deal with a potty-training crisis.

Think about where your food comes from
Ha, easy! Mom could answer that. Dad got the groceries at Aldi again. For supper they would be having Swedish roll-mop herrings with Aldi's award-winning potato chips and a Bulgarian brand of beer. They would be dining in the backyard under the dazzling new outdoor solar lights Dad bought at Target.

EXERCISE:
Meditating with a raisin

1 Sit in a comfortable chair (clear off the cat hair and Playmobil pirates).

2 Hold a raisin in your hand.

3 Look at the raisin as if you have never seen one before (first make sure none of your neighbors can see you).

4 Imagine it growing on the vine (if you start to think "what a waste of a grape," skip this step. You probably need a glass of wine first. Then return to step 1).

5 Be conscious of what you see: its shape, texture, color, size, is it hard or soft? (It's a raisin.)

6 Slowly smell the raisin. (Do raisins even have a smell?)

7 Are you planning to eat the raisin? (No.) Is it difficult not to pop it in your mouth? (I think I can just about resist.)

8   How does the raisin feel? (Does it have
    feelings?) Think about its size.
9   Put the raisin in your mouth. (Remove
    any bits of unwanted fluff.)
10 Bite gently into the raisin. Feel its
    squishiness. (No! I don't want to hurt
    the raisin; heck am I losing my mind?)
11 Sit quietly, breathe, be aware of what
    you sense (try to ignore Dad slipping
    out the door to go running...that is NOT
    scheduled in the family planner).
12 Think, "forget the raisin,
    give me the grape" and
    reach for a bottle of
    Malbec...you'll need
    it to cope with
    the bedtime
    routine.
13 Well done, you
    have completed
    this meditation.
    Pour yourself
    another
    glass.

Nourish your body

After feeding the kids, the dog, and the guinea pig (whose name Mom couldn't remember), and making Dad a quick sandwich for him to enjoy when he got back late from his "business meeting," Mom was too exhausted to eat. So after the bedtime routine she grabbed a large bowl of peanuts and a Kit Kat and washed them down with a big glass of Merlot. The next morning she was up a few pounds—a bit of a mystery as she had skipped supper.

Zen saying: *When you drink, just drink.*
When you walk, just walk.

Mom finds the first one easiest to do.
She loses herself in the clink of the ice as it hits the glass, the splash of clear liquid, the gentle bubbles, the delicious smell of botanical tonic, and the sharp zest of the lemon. She mindfully takes a long, deep drink and gives thanks for all that is Gin & Tonic. Amen.

Eating with impunity

Mom had eaten all of the Almond Joy. The almonds and coconut were fine (good enough for Gwyneth = good enough for Mom), but the chocolate was more difficult to justify and left her with no choice but to go and stand in the corner and think about what she did.

"What about the broccoli? You've only eaten the crispy potato wedges. You need to eat the broccoli to be strong and healthy. Eat just one piece of broccoli please…OK, just the broccoli floret then, maybe one tiny little one just for me. Pleeeease." Dad could be so stubborn.

The joy of cooking

Mom had puréed the s*i*t out of a butternut squash for the baby and was feeling a lot calmer. She had saved a little extra to go in the casserole, which was more than could be said for the wine.

EXERCISE:
Make a daily food journal

A food journal can help you on your path to achieve mindful eating. In the time you have left after you have written the grocery list, bought the groceries, put them away, taken them out again, and then cooked them, take a few quiet moments to ponder and record your experiences.

1 You don't need to write down every time you lick your plate, but you do need to be honest about the kids' leftovers. Those pizza crusts you used to scoop up the last of the hummus do actually count. Just because no one saw you eat them it doesn't mean they are calorie-free.
2 Write down in your journal when you feel hungry. It can't be all the time.
3 Be honest when you suspect you are eating through boredom. Surely your life is more fulfilling than that?
4 Make a note when you reach for unhealthy snacks. A handful of Fruit Loops straight from the box really doesn't count as one of your five-a-day.

It's magic! Before long, you too will
be just like Gwyneth, only without the
humongous bank balance.

Practice rituals, not routines
set by The Regime (a.k.a. Mom)

Ritual (noun): A set of meaningful actions, performed in a set order, to bring about contentment and calm. If we don't practice mindfulness, rituals can often lose their meaning and become mindless routines.

Routine (noun): Something we do repeatedly and automatically, without thought or focus. A routine is a path for mindlessness to enter our lives.

When you do the dishes, really enjoy the privileged moment, thinking only about doing the dishes, the smell of Palmolive Ultra Dish Liquid, Lotus Blossom & Lavender, the playful foam, the wetness of it all. That is a ritual. And the true path to inner happiness.

Really? Really.

Triggers can help

and not just the one on the Nerf gun

Mindfulness trigger (noun): Something to help you break out of autopilot and into spontaneous, more joyful living. A reminder to bring you back to mindfulness, making every daily activity an enjoyable, meditative experience. Except, perhaps, changing the diaper that has leaked all the way up baby's back and into his hair.

EXERCISE:
Create triggers

Write heart-warming messages on sticky notes and stick them up around the house to remind you (every minute of the day) how you should be living your life. It won't be annoying at all. Here are some ideas:

- **Day dreaming is not the answer** and anyway George Clooney is married now.
- **Be grateful for everything around you** even that towering pile of ironing.
- **Live in the now** because you don't have time to do anything else.
- **Tell someone you love them** Come on, you do, really. Don't you?
- **Laugh at one of Dad's jokes**, but only if it's genuinely funny.

If words escape you, just draw a smiley face and stick it on the dishwasher to remind you to be grateful as you empty it for the third time that day.

CHAPTER
2

LEARN
GRATITUDE

and a big fat thank you to me

Thanks a lot

Mindful gratitude (noun): Feeling thankful [for mom], appreciative [of mom] and returning kindness [to mom]. FAMILY PLEASE READ AND TAKE NOTE.

Count your blessings

Every day you dish up a dinner that you lovingly took out of a package, microwaved, and arranged beautifully on the plate for your loved ones…to be met with a wall of silence. Oh the indignity of having to ask if they like it when you know the answer (it is being pushed around the plate and hidden under forks). Or even worse, the pain of having to try to force a loaded spoon into a baby's pursed lips.

It's hard to feel thankful when this scene plays out on a daily basis. But you must silence your inner voice, the one that is screaming "Just f**king eat it, it's not arsenic-laden pig poop, it's highly nutritious pizza with a side serving of well-balanced garden salad!" Instead try a new approach: don't take it personally, pat yourself on the back for getting a lovely meal on the table in good time, and think of all the worms that will benefit from your delicious meal when you turn it into compost. Count your blessings for your family's honesty. So what if they don't like your cooking? If you weren't trying to prove a point, you wouldn't have eaten it either.

EXERCISE:
Mom's daily gratitude journal

To help you on your journey to achieve a state of mindful gratitude, try keeping a daily journal to write down all the little things you have to feel thankful for. Here are some ideas to get you started.

- Your toddler's wonderful art work. She's so creative, such a budding talent. If only she'd use the large stack of paper you have given her, rather than crayoning the walls.
- The tonic hasn't gone flat, despite the fact that you are now buying the extra-large bottles.
- Dad's new-found interest in his health. It's just a shame he leaves his smelly sports gear on the bathroom floor.
- Your children's healthy bowel motions and efforts to go to the bathroom unassisted. You know about this because someone has left a poop in the toilet and peed on the floor. But we all make puddles now and again, don't we Mom?

- The cat is so well behaved. He hasn't crapped on the neighbor's patio for at least a week.
- Hair wash day. The bath is warm and bubbly and smells delicious. Let's hope the neighbors don't hear the blood-curdling howls as you drag a comb through the tangles.
- Your family's thoughtfulness: someone removed the three wizened apricots from the fruit bowl and put them in a nice line next to it.
- Wine (red, white, sparkling, who cares?) and cold, cold beer.
- You survived another day.

Well done Mom!

Mindful giving

When a present is not really a present

Mom was trying really hard to look happy and grateful, but she was fairly sure that a year's subscription to Norton AntiVirus was not on her birthday list. Especially as she knew it would bring a whole world of pain when Dad tried to install it on the family computer.

Cherish the small love tokens your children bring—wilted flowers, yet more interesting stones, half-dead snails, the shamelessly glitzy mother's day necklace. Before too long they will be bringing home unsuitable boyfriends and large phone bills.

Enjoy things while they last. Everything is fleeting. Apart from the laundry basket. That is always there and always bountiful.

Positive affirmations

Mom had silenced her inner critic by wearing her "You are Awesome" T-shirt. It was a bit tight in places and her post-natal bulges misshaped the letters, but it still made her feel all sorts of awesome.

Mom was feeling truly grateful

She had done the scratch-and-sniff on the kids' dirty gym clothes and it definitely all had another wear in it.

EXERCISE:
Don't take things for granted

This exercise will awaken your mind to the good things in your life.

1 Close your eyes and think about all the things you love and value: your slippers, the Gucci bag that you discovered in a Goodwill Superstore, potato chips (any flavor), that new bottle of Cachaca just waiting to be opened, your Chanel lipstick. Oh, and Dad and the kids, of course.

2 Imagine that, one by one, all these things are taken away. Your feet are cold, you're thirsty and hungry and not wearing any lipstick. Experience how awful it is; feel the pain.

3 Then imagine that, one by one, they all come back to you. You feel truly grateful for everything you love (except maybe Dad; there's room for improvement there). Take a moment to savor the warm fuzzy feeling before you once again get down to business.

EXERCISE:
Smile into your body

This exercise is designed to encourage negative thoughts to leave your body.

1 Hold your hands gently together, joining fingers to fingers and thumbs to thumbs (don't worry, there's no complicated leg positioning).
2 Breathe deeply for a few moments (the easy bit).
3 Allow a big smile to form on your lips (go on, you can do it, imagine you have won the lottery and are going to The Maldives on vacation by yourself).
4 Feel the smile flood your body (cell by cell, jiggly bit by jiggly bit, feel the joy spread, it knows no bounds).
5 Now pull yourself together and stop being an ungrateful b*tch.

CHAPTER
3

PRACTICE EMPATHY, COMPASSION & KINDNESS

but don't let the b**tards take advantage

Finding inner kindness

Empathy (noun): to feel others' misfortunes and experience the hurt with them. This is the sign of a true mom. But not a true wife: if it's Dad's misfortune, then it's just plain funny.

Compassion (noun): the next step up from empathy; sympathetic pity; a desire to alleviate others' pain. Like sticking a bandage on a grazed knee, or a cut finger, or that thumb that is starting to go a strange color and is sticking out at a funny angle.

Kindness (noun): acts of humanity and benevolence that make people feel better; like buying your small child ice cream after you accidentally shut their fingers in the car door.

Sharing the pain

It was a whole hour until lunch time and Mom was feeling and hearing her children's hunger pain. But she couldn't give in or they'd never eat their healthy nutrient-packed meal. Thinking only of her children, she snuck to the cupboard, quickly wolfed down that Dark Chocolate Bunny left over from Easter, and disposed of the wrapper unnoticed.

"There, there, you'll be okay. Let me kiss it better." Dad could be such a baby… try childbirth you wimp.

EXERCISE:
Love thyself

How can you love your family if you don't love yourself? This exercise will boost your inner confidence and remind you of your talents and your worth to all those around you.

1 Draw an outline of yourself. It doesn't have to be anatomically correct. (It might help to trace a picture of Angelina Jolie. How come she can look so bloody good after having twins?)

2 Choose two different colored pens: a green one for all the things you like about yourself, and a red one for all the things that need improvement.

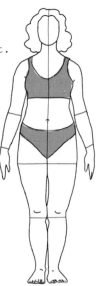

3 Write nice things about yourself using your green pen: "nice eyes," "always happy on a Friday," "kind to the cat."

4 Follow this with your red pen for the things you would like to improve about yourself. This will inspire you to work on them: "voice beginning to sound like my mother's," "eats too many cookies."

5 Make sure there are more green words than red, you loser: this is supposed to be uplifting.

EXERCISE:
Spread joy with random acts of kindness

It need only be a small gesture, but a random act of kindness spreads joy from giver to receiver. Not only will it make you feel smug and saintly, it will also endear you even more to the ones you love. Try to do one good deed each day (if that's not feasible, maybe once a month). Here are some ideas to get you started.

 I Write an inspiring slogan on your child's eraser during exam week: "*You can do it,*" "*Deep breath,*" "*We love you whatever,*" "*Next time do your homework.*"

 2 Don't just think it, say it: "Your garden looks lovely," "I think you are really special," "That dinner was delicious." But keep it appropriate; "Nice butt" isn't something you should tell the plumber.

3 Offer a helping hand: If you see someone you know struggling with their groceries, why not offer to help? But only if it's one bag and they only live next door. Who do they think you are? World's Strongest Woman?

4 Talk to someone while you're shopping who might not get the chance to have a conversation very often: They'll be delighted to hear about your broken washing machine, the repairman who never comes, the enormous pile of ironing you haven't had the inclination to do, the really annoying roadworks on the way to school, the noisy woman next door with the yappy dog, the new diaper design that you. Just. Totally. Can't. Stand.

5 Next time you are making cupcakes, make a few extra to give to an elderly neighbor or friend who has just had a baby. Just get over there right away before your steely will dissolves and you scoff them all while watching *Bridget Jones* for the 14th time.

6 Chat with a new mom at the school gates and invite her for coffee. Surely she'll be desperate to make new friends: Then spend the next six months avoiding eye contact in case she invites you back.

Random acts of kindness to the kids

Who are you kidding? This is a totally unnecessary concept. Your whole life revolves around pleasing the little darlings. If, however, they have been particularly lovely, buy them a comic book and they will think you are the Very Best Mom in the Whole Wide World. For at least five minutes anyway.

Show compassion for Dad

Here are a few ways you can show Dad what he really means to you. Because you love him really and he works *soooo* hard.

- Iron Dad a shirt...the shock might kill him.
- Get in some of his favorite beers. Chill the lagers, warm the ales, and try not to drink them all yourself before he gets home.
- Allow Dad to go to the bathroom without hollering "You can't *still* be in there? How long can it *possibly* take? Put your smartphone down, get out here, and play with these children. You wanted them."
- Give him a compliment in his bag lunch in the form of a pink sticky note with a romantic message, like "sometimes you can be really funny," or "you have gorgeous legs."
- Tell him his beer belly has definitely got a little bit smaller since he's been going to the gym.

Don't get carried away
Dad was puffing and panting and making such a meal of ironing one shirt that Mom nearly took pity on him... but not quite. Just in time she remembered that if she was too nice too often, everyone would take her for granted and that would never do.

EXERCISE:
A loving-kindness meditation

This should help you feel better disposed and more kindly to yourself and to others. Let's see, shall we?

1 Take 15 minutes for yourself in a quiet place (ha, a chance to steal Dad's hiding place…the bathroom).

2 Spray some air freshener around the room to make sure it smells nice. Half a can should do the trick.

3 Get yourself seated comfortably on your throne and imagine yourself as a child who is much loved. Feel the warm glow surround you like a cozy blanket.

4 Repeat the following mantra for seven-and-a-half minutes (in your head, not out loud. That would be weird).

May I be filled with loving-kindness
  (and potato chips and wine).
May I be safe from inner and outer dangers
  (like self-doubt and meteor strikes).
May I be well in body and mind
  (…possibly too late for this one).
May I be at ease and happy
  (and never change another diaper).

5 Once you are feeling better about yourself, then you can think about others (for a change). Think about someone who has helped you (can't think of anyone at the moment, but it will come to you). Do the exercise again, this time repeating a mantra about that person instead, expressing gratitude to them. Something like "thank God for babysitters and on-demand grocery delivery."

Feel your loving juices flow.

3 kindnesses that Mom has never forgotten

1 The lady who let her go to the front of the line when her toddler was about to make a puddle. Although Mom's gratitude diminished a little when the kind lady helpfully pointed out that Mom had barf all over her left shoulder.

2 The senior citizen who gave her a knowing, kind, "we've all been there" nod and smile when her child was lying rigid on the supermarket floor, screaming "*I want ice cream!*" Even if said senior citizen was still there ten minutes later, giving the same kind nod and smile over and over again.

3 The man who, despite having two suitcases of his own, helped Mom get the stroller off the train without launching her sleeping child head-first onto the track. Mom didn't know why he insisted on taking the same end of the stroller as her. It was very awkward squeezing through the narrow train door together, pressed up against each other.

CHAPTER
4

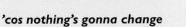

FIND
ACCEPTANCE

'cos nothing's gonna change

Mom-tolerance

Acceptance (noun): Perception and acknowledgment of a situation or thing without judgment. Setting approval or resistance aside and accepting things as they are. Like biting your lip and thanking Dad for taking the kids to the hairdresser's when every part of you is secretly screaming "Why would you even think that giving the kids a No.2 is a good idea? *Especially the girls!*"

Don't call me mom...
It was quite endearing, but Mom wondered if Dad would ever call her anything other than "mom." She had high hopes for "gorgeous," but would happily settle for her actual real name.

What's done *is* done

Let go of the past, you can't change it. That drawing of Barney the Dinosaur scrawled in purple Sharpie permanent marker on the kitchen door is there to stay, for everyone to see. Accept the situation, don't resist. Concentrate on not missing out on the beauty in life. Barney is exquisitely observed, even though he does look a bit phallic.

Banish feelings of inadequacy and look at all the things on your To-Do List simply as interesting hurdles just waiting for you to hurl yourself over.

Expect the worst to avoid disappointment

Let go of those unrealistic expectations and embrace reality. If you are expecting the kids to hang their clothes up in their floordrobe, rather than their wardrobe, you won't be disappointed. In fact, after you have lovingly laundered and ironed their things, you could just roll them up into a ball and throw them on the bedroom floor. That's true, deep acceptance.

EXERCISE:
Be a cat

Cats have got it all figured out. They wander freely unburdened by relationships and chuck their kids out as soon as they can fend for themselves. They spend their days grooming, sleeping, and tormenting small furry animals. They allow someone else to put their dinner in their dish and give them a loving stroke. Despite all this, they treat everyone with absolute scorn. So take a leaf out of a cat's book and start with this cat stretch to release mental and physical tension.

1 Get yourself a yoga (or any other) mat for soft landing in case it all goes horribly wrong.

2 Assume the role of a cat. Get down on all fours, arch your back and stretch out your front paws, pushing your bottom into the air. Feel the tension release right down the length of your body.

3 Roll onto your back, put your legs in the air and see whether you can lick your bum.

4 With a flick of your tail, nonchalantly straighten up and perfect the "I don't give a rat's ass" swagger across the room. If someone offers to tickle your tummy, definitely roll over and accept.

Accepting change

Mom had to accept that her shoe-horizons had shrunk since her feet had expanded. She now had just three pairs in active service: her rubber boots, Converse sneakers, and Birkenstocks. There was no other option but to have each in four shades of gray if she was going to be equipped for every occasion.

Your kids are the reason you wake up every morning…at some unearthly hour, in the dark, to the sound of Pokémon on the DS.

5 things to accept once you are a mom

1 You will be constantly tired, but never bored (you should be so lucky, lucky, lucky, lucky).

2 Your patience will be tested, but you will find inner reserves you never knew you had (the wine glasses are currently languishing at the bottom of the laundry basket).

3 You will be challenged on a daily basis, but those challenges will keep you looking young and on your toes (apart from your face…that will show the strain).

4 You won't often get any appreciation, but you can rest assured that they love you really (well the dog definitely does, when you remember to feed him).

5 One day, when they have kids of their own, they will understand. But you'll be long-gone by then, cruising around the Med like Shirley Valentine.

EXERCISE:
Confronting anger

If acceptance is proving tricky, and you feel anger rising inside you, this useful exercise will get you back on track.

1 Step away from whatever is making you angry. Find a quiet place to sit (be inventive, but be aware that they will seek you out wherever you hide).
2 Root your feet firmly on the floor, allowing your bottom to support your weight (hell yeah, thank goodness for a sturdy bottom). Rest your hands in your lap and let your face hang loose. Wobble those jowls like you just don't care.
3 Allow your body to breathe by itself (has it not been doing that quite successfully for the last however many years?). Feel the breaths entering and leaving your body (yes it's definitely going in and out, on repeat…you are definitely alive, but still angry).

4 Now approach your anger, acknowledge its existence, find words to express it, observe the feelings pent up inside you. If you are bored or bemused by now that's good. You have probably forgotten what you were angry about…job done!

5 Talk to your anger and tell it where to go. Explain that you're not going to let it control you anymore, then release it and envisage it floating away like a helium balloon in a light breeze.

6 If it is a stubborn little b**tard and won't get lost, go back into the living room, lie down on the floor, and have a full-blown tantrum. It seems to work for the kids.

Accept that your purse will never be the same again

It was once a designer item of covetable loveliness with a beautiful lining and space for nothing more than a cellphone, a Chanel lipstick, and a pocket mirror. Now it contains the following:

1 Sticky, congealed candies

2 Crushed cookie crumbs

3 An old energy bar wrapper

4 Several old crayons that have stained the bag's lining

5 A pack of ancient, dried-out hand wipes

6 A dead flower

7 A snail shell

8 Half an emergency candy bar, covered with hair

9 Unidentified pieces of plastic from a Kinder Joy egg

10 Drugstore makeup (a gift from Dad)

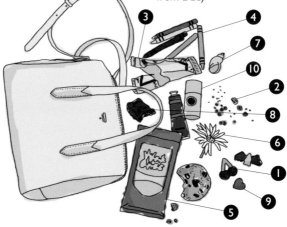

ACCEPTING THE LAW OF THE SMALL CHILD

Stroller

I am small child. I will go completely rigid and scream. I will arch my back so you can't do the straps up.

I am small child. I will go all floppy just to spite you, so you can't get me out of my chariot again.

That is the way it is, so deal with it.

Getting ready to go out

I am small child. I will shut my mouth so you can't clean my teeth.

I will scream like you are trying to kill me if you bring a brush within an inch of my hair. Don't think I will wear shoes, I only ever wear rubber boots (without socks).

Bedtime

I will not drink all day, despite your best efforts to keep me hydrated. I will, however, at bedtime have to have at least three drinks on demand, followed by no fewer than seven trips to the bathroom. That is the law and if you don't abide I will delay your wine time even further by screaming.

Accept the bedtime dilemma

You are exhausted and desperate to collapse under a blanket but you're also crying out for a child-free evening of wine and box-set heaven. Bed or box set... which is it to be? Sometimes the next-day pain just has to be weathered in exchange for those precious moments on the sofa with Daniel Craig/Ryan Gosling (delete and replace as appropriate).

Your time will come

Acceptance is easier to practice if you know, at some
time in the future, you will be repaid for your efforts
(like when Dad finally offers to do the midnight feed).
Take lots of embarrassing photographs of your children
at every stage of their lives: first poop on the potty; naked
and smeared with chocolate; first day at kindergarten
(what's that dark stain on his pants?). Revenge can be
yours at their 21st birthday party or wedding. It's just a
matter of planning ahead and seizing the day with your
overhead projector and meticulously prepared slide show.

CHAPTER
5

RESERVE
JUDGMENT

don't even THINK it

Judge and thou shalt be judged

Judgment (noun): An opinion, conclusion, or assumption formed in the light of available evidence. Many thoughts that enter our heads are judgmental: judgmental of ourselves and judgmental of others. Do not pursue these negative thoughts. Observe them, acknowledge them, then let them go. Except the funny ones; it's only okay to share these with your best friend.

The joy of playgroup

Mom would never have guessed that hanging out in a dark and dusty church hall with a load of tired mothers, hyperactive children, and unhygienic toys could become the highlight of her week. With a weak cup of coffee and a sugar cookie in her hand, Mom was trying not to judge, really. She was doing well until circle sing time. She really wished that the "Wheels On the Bus" would just f**king fall off.

If you make assumptions about other moms before you really know them, you might be the one to miss out. Who knows? They might offer to babysit one day.

Thou shalt not judge other moms

Unless they are wearing Lycra *and* sporting yoga mats (surely carrying all your kids' schoolbags is exercise enough?). Or unless they are hanging around the school gates blocking the paths of the moms who are in a rush to get to work. Try to give them the benefit of the doubt. They might be discussing important things LIKE HOW IT MIGHT BE THEIR TURN NEXT YEAR TO ORGANIZE THE SCHOOL F**KING BAKE SALE.

If you are comfortable in your own life,
you will be less concerned about the
lives of others…Slippers on!

Avoid judging the neighbors

How dare the attractive, young people next door have
a moving-in party, with their cool friends, until the
early hours of the morning, with cold beers, on-trend
music, and long, absorbing conversations…how utterly
inconsiderate of them to enjoy their lives. The b**tards
are keeping everyone awake with their enthusiasm for
life and their damn youth.

If your children have your attention,
a safe place to sleep, and something to eat
every day, then you are a good mom.
Even if you do an air punch when
you've got them into bed.

EXERCISE:

Remove those judgment specs
(But best keep your beer goggles on)

Thoughts are constantly popping into our minds throughout the day and night, many of them negative and judgmental about ourselves. These thoughts can become a chorus of self-criticism and blame. Only by freeing ourselves from them can we grow calmer and more present. This exercise can (or cannot) help.

1 Imagine you are seeing life through dirty glasses which are distorting your view of yourself and your life. Now imagine you are removing those glasses. Suddenly you see things with a fresh eye (damn, this house is dirty; is that what Dad really looks like?).

2 Allow harsh self-judgments to melt like a warm candy bar and accept yourself and your actions without criticism, unburdened by tainted views (is that Milky Way, Baby Ruth, or Hershey's?).

3 Feel compassion and deep understanding for yourself. Acknowledge that you are trying your best in difficult circumstances. (Who wouldn't be snarky, bad-tempered, and bitter if they had to put up with what you have to?)

4 Feel the burden of self-doubt lifting. You now see just how awesome you are. (And recognize just whose fault it is that you have become this way. You are surrounded by ungrateful human beings.)

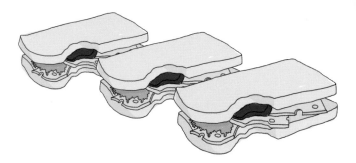

Don't judge yourself too harshly

Don't feel badly if you serve the kids grilled cheese sandwiches three nights in a row. Just add some ketchup tomorrow and call it a pizza sandwich. And if you put a dill pickle on the side of the plate, you can put a check mark in the "well-balanced meal" box too. Well done! Scurvy won't set in for at least another week.

Don't be SanctiMOMious

Not all pain can be seen, so the next time you make a judgment about the skinny b**ch at the school gates, remember that she has feelings too. She may be hiding all sorts of pain behind that slim, attractive, carefully groomed exterior.

MAKE YOUR WISHES CLEAR

It's not fair to pass judgment on others using your
own set of inner rules. You have to let them know
what you expect or they can never conform.
It can help to write it down, so everyone is clear.
Leave a helpful note in the changing bag and,
once more, harmony will reign and your
minds will be but one.

Rules of the changing bag
(Yup. This means you DAD)

1 Always replace the diaper once you've used it.

2 Always replace the diaper sack once
you have used it.

3 Always replace the wet wipes if you
have used them all.

4 Always replace the lid on the rash cream
PROPERLY after you have used it.

Failure to comply will result in me leaving a
shitty diaper under your pillow.

CHAPTER
6

RESTORE
INNER PEACE

*or at least have a stab
at outer peace*

Peace be with you

Peace (noun): Freedom from disturbance, serenity, tranquility. Something that Mom last experienced one Saturday five years ago, before the arrival of her bundles of joy, when Dad went out to play golf.

> Come on inner peace,
> I don't have all day!

5 ways to find peace among the chaos

1 Hang up the laundry to dry. If you get tired, it's perfectly acceptable to have a little rest on the laundry line (check first it will take your weight).

2 Hand over the baby to Dad the minute he walks through the door. Don't let him take his coat or shoes off.

3 Spend a very long time cooking dinner and arranging the beans on the toast. "See how busy I am making this marvelous dinner for my family."

4 Wrestle the barbecue from Dad and spend an hour every Saturday just watching the flames, swigging beer, and turning sausages from time to time.

5 Declutter your closet. Make several piles— Goodwill Services, mend, keep—then light the mother of all bonfires to destroy the large pile of size zeros that mocks you every time you go to get dressed.

The true path to serenity

The only way to experience true serenity when you
have small children is to get a job like Dad. You will look
clean and presentable every day, read a book during
your commute, operate your brain cells, talk to adults,
have them listen to you, gain the respect of your peers,
and enjoy a whole half-hour's lunch break completely to
yourself…with *sushi* and the MSNBC News. It'll be chaos
when you get home, but it'll have been worth it.

EXERCISE:
Finding ultimate peace

Try this unusual exercise to help you find peace in your chaotic life. It might seem a little unfamiliar at first but, with practice, you will slowly learn and develop the skills to master it.

1 Tell Dad you are having a nap.
2 Lock yourself in the bedroom.
3 Lie down on the bed.
4 Go to sleep for an hour.
5 Get up refreshed.

How the hell could she find inner peace when she couldn't even find her house keys?

A peaceful night

The baby was in her own bed. Joy knew no bounds. Mom and Dad had their king-size bed back to themselves. Or at least Dad did. Mom was hanging over the edge of the cramped single bed, her arm around the baby, without so much as a corner of the blanket. Even the toys in the bed had a better deal than her, all 12 of them. But at least the little one was sleeping and so was Dad—she could hear his peaceful snores and it warmed her cold feet and heart.

A peaceful visualization

This meditative technique can help you on your path to peace and tranquility. Close your eyes and imagine you are on a plane, jetting off to a beautiful tropical island where you plan to spend a whole month in utter bliss. Your delightful children are busy with "snax" and complimentary toy airplanes, so you are confident this will be a serene, enjoyable flight. The attendant has just poured your second gin and tonic. It's all going so well…until the baby in the front row begins to scream.

CHAPTER
7

REDISCOVER ADVENTURE

once you've emptied the dishwasher

Broaden your horizons

Adventure (noun): a new, daring, or risky activity. Like impulsively chucking out your maternity baggies, before checking to see if you can squeeze your muffin top into your skinnies. Rediscovering adventure can bring meaning back to your existence and rekindle your zest for life.

Mix up the routine

Mom was looking forward to the sun going down because, for once, Dad was going to read the bedtime story. Mom knew Dad would fall asleep too, leaving her with the remote control and that family-size bag of M&Ms all to herself.

EXERCISE:
Even the mundane can be exhilarating

If you can't face trekking in the Himalayas with a newborn, take some risks closer to home. You may still experience that frisson of excitement.

1 Next time you go shopping, try Kmart instead of Aldi.
2 Play a game of Spot the New Product… "Ooh look! Ella's Kitchen have brought out a new Fruit Pouch! Excited.com."
3 Throw some different ingredients into your basket (go wild and buy a white, sliced loaf of bread, the cheapest you can find. The kids will love you for it).
4 Go clockwise around the stop instead of counterclockwise. That'll irritate all the other shoppers. Tip: a last-minute swerve with the cart is always particularly adrenaline-raising.
5 Get home and realize that there is nothing in your shopping bag that will produce a balanced meal (unless, of course, sour cream and onion potato chips count as a vegetable).

Mom was ready to embrace the new…

She had waited in all day with a small wailing child but
finally her delivery had arrived. She delighted over the
beautiful packaging, tenderly unfolded the tissue paper, and
there they were, things of beauty. Her new cream-colored,
calf skin, high-heeled clogs—simple and totally stylish.
What a shame she would never wear them. (Are you
nuts? Outside? They'd be ruined!) But they really were
lovely and would look just perfect sitting there on
the bedroom floor.

An adventure *en famille*

It was the first big family vacation and everyone was
together on the plane, heading off into the unknown.
Dad had put his earphones in and was already engrossed
in *Resident Evil: The Final Chapter*. Although Mom was
faced with eight hours of childcare alone, she chuckled to
herself. She had "forgotten" to pack Dad's cellphone, his
Kindle, his iPad, and his laptop. This was the last screen
he would see for three weeks.

New Year, new you

You know the feeling, the one that is nagging in your head, the one that can't be put off any longer…the one that says you *need to do some exercise*. Getting into your Lycra and working out after having a baby is like the first time you jump back in the sack…painful but necessary. All those inspiring blogs and books agree that thinking about it is worse than actually doing it. Don't you believe a word of it. All lies. It is as bad as you think…big mirrors, bright lights, physically fit people, and sheer sweaty, painful exhaustion to be endured in the vain hope that you might lose a few pounds and manage to get to the top of the stairs without having an asthma attack. If you think it's going to be horrible, it'll be much, much worse. If you need inspiration, get this. if you do some exercise (even a little bit) you can justify a large glass of wine and a party size bag of Lay's potato chips to help you through the bedtime routine.

SMALL CHANGES

If you are less about life-endangering stunts and more about gently broadening your horizons, here are some little things you can try to stop you from boring yourself, and everyone around you, to death:

- Switch the Pinot Grigio for Pinot Noir.
- Wear a summer scarf in January. You rebel.
- Say yes to the next five questions that come your way (within reason).
- Go fruit picking. Not to go all domestic goddess and make jam, silly, but to infuse your booze. *Note: you have to wait for it to infuse before you can drink it.*
- Eat outside in the backyard, even when it's cold. But sit on a cushion to avoid hemorrhoids.
- Change your earrings (if the little princess hasn't lost them all in the toy box).
- Get an undercut. It's a hairstyle.
- Wind down the windows and turn up the volume on your car radio.

- Wear some high heels when you drop off the kids at school, just to show you have some and you can still get your swollen feet into them. Try not to hobble.

Confront your fears

Mom's comfort zone was nowhere to be seen and she was painfully present on the chair lift. Next challenge: getting off the chair lift with dignity intact, followed by trying to get to the bottom of a slippery mountain on two flat sticks. Matters were only made worse by the little one whizzing past her like a pro. At least there was the prospect of the *après ski*…but it would take more than a small (okay, large) Chocolate Chantilly Cream with a double shot of brandy to bring joy on this vacation.

3 new things for the kids to try

1 Being nice to Mom (she is actually really nice beneath her grumpy exterior).

2 Being nice to Mom (she loves every square inch of you and only wants the best for you).

3 Being nice to Mom (you know what'll happen if you're not; you've been warned).

3 new things for Mom to try

1 Being nice to Mom seven days a week (because you're worth it).

2 Being nice to Dad at least one day a week (because he's almost worth it).

3 Not getting mad seven days a week. Save it all up for a massive blowout at a Boxercise class… the gloves are off.

CELEBRATE YOUR LIFE

any excuse for a party

We are (still) family

Celebrate (verb): To give thanks for something, to mark an occasion with an enjoyable activity, to have a reason to get loaded with family and friends. Mainly involves endless lists, lots of shopping, and too much booze, followed by a day of suffering under the blankets while the kids take full advantage by jumping on your head, spending hours watching TV, and raiding the treats cupboard. This is followed by a week of worrying about whom you might have offended, recycling empty bottles, and finding popcorn in strange places, like your underpants.

It's not just a kid's party…

Thank goodness the little one had chosen a superhero party. Finally everyone would see that Mom was Wonder Woman. Even if she had to don her bathing suit and rubber boots to make them all realize it.

EXERCISE:
Celebrate your every breath

There's always a reason to celebrate. If you are breathing, then you are alive. And if that isn't cause for cracking open the leftover Christmas Prosecco, then what is? Try this exercise when you know you are probably alive but you don't feel it.

1 Breathe deeply and slowly, drawing the breaths out as long as you can. Focus on your inhale, and then on your exhale. Be curious about your breathing. (Hello there breathing. How are you today?)
2 Celebrate and rediscover your joy for life through your breath. Make sure you clean your teeth first, though. You won't find joy if you can smell last night's southern fried chicken.
3 Now breathe even deeper and hold your breath for a count of five before you exhale. Come on, don't just do it, do it like your life depends on it.
4 Now you are really living (apparently).

Christmas…a time to give thanks

Christmas is a time of peace and joy for all men (men being the operative word). There was no peace for Mom. She had started making lists in September. She had spent three months shopping for presents, and another week for the food; she spent a week writing cards (and still didn't get manage to mail them in time for Christmas). All Dad had to do was get the Christmas tree out of the attic, put his reindeer sweater on, and turn up. How lovely and considerate that he had wrapped his presents for her so beautifully, using up all of her carefully selected, coordinated gift-wrapping paper.

Small successes bring great joy…

Mom had long given up on the big things, but was concentrating on small, everyday successes as a path to happiness. To celebrate baby pooping in the potty, she gave

THE PERFECT HYGGE KIT

him a Hershey's chocolate kiss. To celebrate her efforts
to get him this far, she gave herself the rest of the bag.

Well done Mom!

Mom thought Scandinavian culture might have the
answers to her woes so she decided to celebrate her
birthday *hygge* style. She would need a few key items:

- Scented candle (not vomit-inducing vanilla, though).
- Cashmere socks, wrapped in tissue paper…living
  the dream.
- A good book. Or maybe just a magazine with lots
  of pictures. Mom thinks she might have lost the
  power of reading through brain shrivelage.
- An entire bag of snack-size Mounds candy bars
  (none of that expensive grown-up salted caramel,
  70 percent cocoa solids stuff…just some good old
  shredded coconut filling coated in dark chocolate).
- A mug of hot chocolate, in case the Mounds don't
  provide Mom without enough of a chocolate hit.

Celebrate what your body can do through exercise

Mom was going to start small by getting to the top of the stairs without a break. Once she had mastered that, the next challenge would be to get all the grocery bags in from the car all at once. After all, a journey of a million miles starts with just one step, then a chocolate chip cookie break, just for some energy.

1 Jog with stroller.
2 Squat next to stroller.
3 Lunge against stroller.
4 Freestyle. Freestyle.

EXERCISE:
Make a reward chart

A little reward can motivate you to strive harder and offers a great way to celebrate your successes. Make an inspiring chart to display on the wall (no stickers required). You'll never want to sit down with your feet up again.

Success	Reward
1 load of laundry –	1 chocolate
3 loads of laundry –	1 bar of chocolate
cleaning out the filter on the dishwasher –	10 minutes of crap TV
2 hours of housework	trip to coffee shop for cake (no kids)
1 hour playing monsters with the kids –	long nap in a darkened room

10 small things worth celebrating with a cocktail

1 Clean bedsheets…crisp, white, and wrinkle-free, until the kids set up a camp under them.
2 Ready-mixed cocktails…why has it taken so long?
3 7 P.M.: Couch, wine, Netflix.
4 A sleeping baby…don't wake the baby making a racket with the cocktail shaker.
5 Grandparents…a marvelous invention, long may they live.
6 Holding an adult conversation uninterrupted… even if it's just a short one. ("What day do the garbagemen come?" "Thursday." CHECK.)
7 The holy trinity—gin, potato chips, and chocolate.
8 Taking a pee alone, uninterrupted by man, small child, or animal.
9 Reading a newspaper or news online for more than five minutes.
10 Clean hair all around. High five!

EXERCISE:
Hurray for me

This exercise will make you feel good about yourself. After all, just being YOU is a cause for celebration.

1 Stand up (this way there's no danger of dropping off to sleep).
2 Close your eyes and imagine you are winning a race. Throw your hands in the air, your best jazz hands, and celebrate as you cross the line first with a loud *"Wooo-hooo!"*
3 Now head straight for the booze.

Share your celebrations with others...

Mom was making some triple chocolate muffins to celebrate her birthday in the office. It was about time those thin girls put on some weight. That would wipe the judgmental smiles off their skinny faces.

CHAPTER
9

RECONNECT WITH THE WORLD

let's add more to the To-Do List

Hello world! It's me, Mom!

Reconnect (verb): To re-establish a bond. To feel something you had stopped feeling (like anything below the waist), to join to something you've been separated from (like your social life), to improve a relationship (which requires Dad getting back from work on time).

The first trip out

After six weeks indoors with your newborn, you emerge into the harsh daylight and head for the grocery store. Bleary-eyed and disoriented, you wonder how you will manage. If you get as far as aisle three without the baby having a meltdown, you should feel proud of yourself. Your mission? To return home with the four items essential to life as you know it: coffee, cake, wipes, and diapers. If you have these in your basket, you will live to fight another day.

FIND YOUR TRIBE

You pushed a baby out of your undercarriage, so you have automatic membership to the Sisterhood of Moms. But finding your own personal tribe is essential if you are going to survive everything that a child will throw at you (literally). These women, if chosen carefully, will pull you through all the s**t that comes your way and have your back, no matter what. These are the six best moms to have in your arsenal:

- **The Chill-out Mom:** "It's just a phase. Don't worry about it."
- **The Baking Mom:** "I've just made a carrot cake with cream cheese frosting. Come on over."
- **The Fun Mom:** "I've booked a table for eight at the new gin bar up the road. Then we can all go back to my place for a Chinese takeout."
- **The Practical Mom:** "It's just mastitis. Hurts like h*ll, but you have to keep feeding."
- **The Fierce Mom:** "Yeah! We're feeding our babies right here. What you gonna do about it?"
- **The Next-best-thing-to-family Mom:** She's always got the coffee ready, a listening ear, and a sturdy shoulder on which to rest a weary head.

GOING BACK TO WORK

An ironed silk shirt, new breast pads, and you're ready for your first week back after maternity leave.

Monday: The first day goes well, you meet people and even remember some of their names. You stay awake through meetings and hold your own.

Tuesday: The in-tray is filling up but you're getting things done, writing presentations, and everything is under control.

Wednesday: You have deadlines to meet but your child wakes up with a runny nose…is it just a sniffle or is it the flu? Definitely a sniffle. A spoon of medication for small child, then drop him off at the nursery when it's busy so runny nose won't be noticed. Arrive at desk to four missed calls, turn the ringer off, and hide in the restroom. Return the call: apparently small child is on deathbed and infecting all other small children with life-threatening snot.

Cancel all work commitments, head home deflated. Pick up small, sickly child, who suddenly comes back to life the minute he gets home and demands to play superheroes. Grrr!

Thursday: Watch 24 episodes of *Sesame Street*

Friday: Watch another 24 episodes of *Sesame Street*.

Come on weekend...

Three years of baby talk had stood Mom
in good stead for the board meeting.

Set up a secret moms' club at work

All members must have graced the office with a slowly
expanding wet patch of breast milk on the front of
their shirt and had to dry off under the hand dryer
in the restroom.

Schedule a date night

They had a found a night that they could both be there.
The babysitter had arrived, milk had been expressed, and
a table was booked in town. Now all they had to do was
muster some enthusiasm and enjoy each other's company.
It was a slow start but, after a few drinks, they were
invincible and could have stayed out all night.

Mom's breasts had other ideas.

SEE YOU AT THE BAR

If all else fails, here are four easy cocktails you can make, even when half asleep. Guaranteed to soothe mind and body. No cocktail shaker necessary.

Negroni Pour a large splash of gin over ice, add a splash of Campari, and one of red vermouth. Top off with soda and a slice of orange.

Dry Martini A chilled glass is a must. Swirl it with vermouth, then drain. Add 3 shots of gin, and an olive. Must be drunk cold (i.e. quickly).

Gin Rickey Ice in a glass, 2 shots of gin, juice of a lime, top off with soda and a wedge of lime.

Sloe Gin Sling Splash some sloe gin in a tall glass, a big squeeze of lemon juice, ice, and soda to top off. Added fruit and mint, optional.

Whew! That's better.

For the E17 moms: Becky, Rachel, Leisa, Helen, Jo, Madeleine, Carole, Mel, and Ness. For Jenny at Blackhorse Road Playgroup, always there with a hug, a cookie, and a cup of tea, and Ruth at Low Hall, a calm, kind presence who made all the difference.

But mostly for my mom, who would come at the drop of a hat with her Mary Poppins bag of tricks and stay for as long as it took for the wind to change.

A Hachette UK Company
www.hachette.co.uk

First published in Great Britain in 2018 by Spruce, a division of Octopus Publishing Group Ltd, Carmelite House, 50 Victoria Embankment, London EC4Y 0DZ
www.octopusbooks.co.uk
www.octopusbooksusa.com

Copyright © Octopus Publishing Group 2018

Distributed in the US by Hachette Book Group, 1290 Avenue of the Americas, 4th and 5th Floors, New York, NY 10104

Distributed in Canada by Canadian Manda Group, 664 Annette St., Toronto, Ontario, Canada M6S 2C8

ISBN 978-1-84601-558-8

A CIP catalog record for this book is available from the British Library.

Printed and bound in China.

10 9 8 7 6 5 4 3 2 1

Commissioning Editor Romilly Morgan
Senior Editor Leanne Bryan
Art Director Juliette Norsworthy
Copy Editor Jo Smith
Americanizer Constance Novis
Designer Sally Bond
Illustrator Agnes Bicocchi
Senior Production Manager Peter Hunt

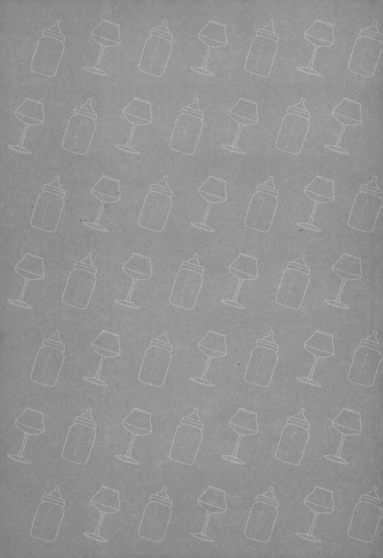